Heinemann First
ENCYCLOPEDIA

Volume 9
Pen-Roo

Heinemann Library
Chicago, Illinois

Customer Service   888–454–2279

Visit our website at www.heinemannlibrary.com

Series Editors: Rebecca and Stephen Vickers, Gianna Williams
Author Team: Rob Alcraft, Catherine Chambers, Sabrina Crewe, Jim Drake, Fred Martin, Angela Royston, Jane Shuter, Roger Thomas, Rebecca Vickers, Stephen Vickers

This revised and expanded edition produced for Heinemann Library by Discovery Books.
Photo research by Katherine Smith and Rachel Tisdale
Designed by Keith Williams, Michelle Lisseter, and Gecko
Illustrations by Stefan Chabluk and Mark Bergin

Originated by Ambassador Litho Limited
Printed in China by WKT Company Limited

10 09 08 07 06
10 9 8 7 6 5 4 3 2

Library of Congress Cataloging-in-Publication Data

Heinemann first encyclopedia.
    p.   cm.
   Summary: A fourteen-volume encyclopedia covering animals, plants, countries, transportation, science, ancient civilizations, US states, US presidents, and world history
    ISBN 1-4034-7116-9 (v. 9 : lib. bdg.)
    1. Children's encyclopedias and dictionaries.
I. Heinemann Library (Firm)
AG5.H45 2005
031—dc22   2005006176

Acknowledgments
Cover: Cover photographs of a desert, an electric guitar, a speedboat, an iceberg, a man on a camel, cactus flowers, and the Colosseum at night reproduced with permission of Corbis. Cover photograph of the Taj Mahal reproduced with permission of Digital Stock. Cover photograph of an x-ray of a man reproduced with permission of Digital Vision. Cover photographs of a giraffe, the Leaning Tower of Pisa, the Statue of Liberty, a white owl, a cactus, a butterfly, a saxophone, an astronaut, cars at night, and a circuit board reproduced with permission of Getty Images/Photodisc. Cover photograph of Raglan Castle reproduced with permission of Peter Evans; J. Allan Cash Ltd., pp. 7, 18, 23, 33 left, 43 bottom; Ardea London Ltd., D. Porer and F. Parer-Cook, p. 15 bottom; C. Beresford/Beresford/Getty Images, p. 47; Trevor Clifford Photography, p. 14; The Hutchison Library/Robert Francis, p. 8; The Hutchison Library, p. 40 top; Bernard Gerard, p. 6 bottom; Hulton Archive/Getty Images, p. 46; Stephen Jaffe/AFP/Getty Images, p. 16; Kathie Atkinson, p. 11; G.I. Bernard, p. 10 top; C. Borland/PhotoLink, p. 39; Tom and Pat Leeson, p. 21 bottom; Tom McHugh, p. 15 top; Richard Packwood, p. 19 right; H. Schwind, p. 10 bottom; S. Solum/PhotoLink, p. 5; Vanessa Vick, p. 19 left; Popperfoto, p. 17; Redferns/Chris Blackwell, p. 6 top; Grant Davis, p. 20 bottom; David Redfern, p. 20 top; Science Photo Library, pp. 4 bottom, 12; Tony Stone Worldwide/Chad Ehlers, p. 4 top; Zefa/Thomas Braise, p. 22 bottom; Bruce Coleman Ltd./Dr Eckart Pott, p. 29 top; EPS Press, p. 32 bottom; Kobal Collection, p. 42 top; Mansell Collection, p. 32 top; Natural History Museum/Mary Anning, p. 25; Oxford Scientific Films/Harold Taylor Abipp, p. 29 bottom; G.I. Bernard, p. 29 bottom; Warren Faidley, p. 34 bottom; Carol Farnetti, p. 35 bottom; David Fritts, p. 38 bottom; Peter Gathercole, p. 40 bottom; Howard Hall, p. 36 bottom; Zig Leszczynski, p. 30 bottom; C.K. Lorenz, p. 30 top; T.C. Middleston, p. 43 top; Sean Morris, p. 33 right; William Paton, p. 29 top; Press-Tige Pictures, p. 35 bottom; Taxi/Ron Chapple, p. 22 top; Steve Turner, p. 38 top; Babs and Bert Wells, p. 37 bottom; Picturepoint, p. 27 bottom; John Mead, p. 31 top; Still Pictures/John Concalori, p. 37 top; Tony Stone Worldwide/Simeone Huber, p. 28; Gavriel Jecan, p. 44; Werner Forman Archive. p. 27 top; Zefa, p. 41 bottom.

Every effort has been made to contact copyright holders of any material reproduced in this book. Any omissions will be rectified in subsequent printings if notice is given to the Publisher.

Welcome to
Heinemann First Encyclopedia

What is an encyclopedia?

An encyclopedia is an information book. It gives the most important facts about many different subjects. This encyclopedia has been written for children who are using an encyclopedia for the first time. It covers many of the subjects from school and others you may find interesting.

What is in this encyclopedia?

In this encyclopedia, each topic is called an *entry*. There is one page of information for every entry. The entries in this encyclopedia explain

- animals
- plants
- dinosaurs
- countries
- geography
- history
- world religions
- music
- art
- transportation
- science
- technology
- states
- famous Americans

How to use this encyclopedia

This encyclopedia has thirteen books called *volumes*. The first twelve volumes contain entries. The entries are all in alphabetical order. This means that Volume 1 starts with entries that begin with the letter A and Volume 12 ends with entries that begin with the letter Z. Volume 13 is the index volume. It also has other interesting information.

Here are two entries that show you what you can find on a page:

This is the letter that the entry starts with.

Fact boxes give you details about the topic.

The "see also" line tells you where to find other related information.

Did You Know? *boxes have fun or interesting bits of information.*

The Fact File *tells you important facts and figures.*

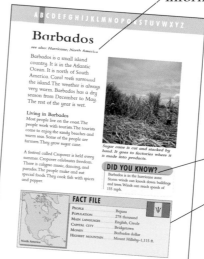

Peninsula

see also: Coast

A peninsula is a narrow piece of land. It sticks out into a body of water like a finger. It has water almost all the way around. It is joined to the mainland. Some peninsulas are very big. Most of the country of Italy is a long peninsula. Italy juts out into the Mediterranean Sea. A peninsula can also be much smaller. It can be less than a half mile long.

How a peninsula is made

Most peninsulas are hard rock. Water wears away the soft land. Hard rock is left behind. It takes thousands of years to wear away the land.

Peninsulas and people

Some people who live on peninsulas are fishermen and women. Peninsulas are also popular places for vacations by the sea. People enjoy the coastlines.

The Baja California peninsula in Mexico has many vacation resorts.

This is a satellite picture of the peninsula called Cape Cod in Massachusetts.

DID YOU KNOW?

The world's largest peninsula is Arabia. It is surrounded on three sides by water.

SOME WORLD PENINSULAS

Scandinavian peninsula.. Europe
Iberian peninsula......... Europe
Brittany peninsula....... Europe
Yucatan peninsula........ Central America
Kamchatka Peninsula.... Asia
Alaska Peninsula .... North America

Pennsylvania

see also: Liberty Bell, United States of America

Pennsylvania is a state in the northeastern United States of America. The Appalachian Mountains stretch across the state from the southwest to the northeast. On either side, the land slopes down. The land in southeast Pennsylvania is good for farming. The northwest tip of the state is on Lake Erie. Summers are warm and winters are cool.

Harrisburg is the state capital.

DID YOU KNOW?

Amish and Mennonite people live in Lancaster County, Pennsylvania. They are religious communities. Some groups have no electricity or telephones in their homes.

In the past

Philadelphia is the largest city in the state. It was an important city in colonial America. The Declaration of Independence was signed there in 1776. Many visitors come to Pennsylvania every year to visit historic sites.

Life in Pennsylvania

Pennsylvania is an important center of industry. Factory workers produce steel and metal products. They also make chemicals, medicines, and food products. The biggest chocolate factory in the world is at Hershey, Pennsylvania.

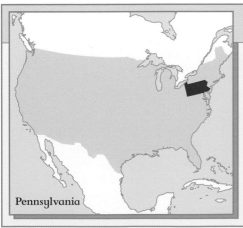

Pennsylvania

FACT FILE

BECAME A STATE... 1787 (2nd state)

LAND AREA......... 44,817 square miles
(32nd largest land area)

POPULATION 12,365,455
(6th most populated state)

OTHER NAME ...... Keystone State

CAPITAL CITY ...... Harrisburg

Percussion Instrument

see also: Music, Musical Instrument, Orchestra

Percussion instruments are musical instruments. They make a sound when they are hit or shaken. Drums, cymbals, gongs, bells, rattles, and wood blocks are all percussion instruments. The very first percussion instruments were people's hands and feet. They were used to make clapping and stamping sounds.

DID YOU KNOW?

The piano is a percussion instrument. Tiny hammers hit tightly-stretched wires when the piano keys are played.

Drummers from the Tutsi tribe from Rwanda in Africa are drumming together.

The drum set is a percussion instrument used in rock, pop, jazz, and some classical music.

TYPES OF PERCUSSION INSTRUMENTS

Drums These are made by stretching something across a hollow box. The drum is hit with a stick or the hands.

Found percussion instruments These are natural objects with their own special sounds. A living tree can be hit with a stick. Two rocks can be tapped together.

Metal percussion instruments These include gongs, cymbals, bells, and tambourines. Some of these are played with sticks or beaters. Others are played by shaking or crashing them together.

Wooden percussion instruments These are often hollow wooden boxes. They make a sharp clicking or booming sound when they are hit.

Peru

see also: Incas, South America

Peru is a country in northwest South America. There is lowland along the coast. The Andes Mountains are inland. There is high flat land and Lake Titicaca in the south. Earthquakes and active volcanoes sometimes kill people and make buildings collapse.

Living in Peru

Farmers grow potatoes, rice, and sugar. Some raise sheep, llamas, and alpacas. The alpaca has very fine wool. Almost three-fourths of the people live and work in towns and cities.

Most Peruvians are Roman Catholic Christians. They celebrate religious festivals at Easter and on saints' days. Many festivals come from the Native American cultures of Peru. People celebrated these festivals with dancing, music, and masks. Music is played on pan pipes and flutes. Some tourists visit the remains of ancient Inca cities.

This woman from the Quéchua tribe in the Andes is weaving belts.

DID YOU KNOW?

The red and white colors in the flag of Peru stand for red and white flamingos.

South America

FACT FILE

PEOPLE	Peruvians
POPULATION	about 27 million
MAIN LANGUAGES	Spanish, Quéchua
CAPITAL CITY	Lima
MONEY	Sol
HIGHEST MOUNTAIN	Huascarán—22,213 feet
LONGEST RIVER	Ucayali River—1,428 miles

Philippines

see also: Asia

The Philippines is a country in southeast Asia. It is made up of many islands. The main islands have mountains and river valleys. The climate is hot. Every year there are heavy rains called monsoons.

Living in the Philippines

About half the people live in the rural areas. In some villages, the community lives in a wooden "long house." This house is raised above the ground. Farmers grow rice, sugar cane, corn, pineapples, and coconuts. A favorite food in the Philippines is *siopao.* It is a kind of dumpling filled with minced meat.

The Philippines is the only country in Asia where most of the people are Christians. This is because Spanish missionaries came to the Philippines more than 450 years ago.

These are women of the Ifugo tribe. The area where they live is known for its terraces where rice is grown.

DID YOU KNOW?

Basketball is the most popular sport in the Philippines. There are also two special Filipino games. *Arnis* is a kind of sword-fighting played with wooden sticks. *Sipa* is a game that is like volleyball.

Asia

FACT FILE

PEOPLE	Filipinos
POPULATION	about 86 million
MAIN LANGUAGES	Pilipino (Tagalog), English
CAPITAL CITY	Manila
MONEY	Philippine peso
HIGHEST MOUNTAIN	Mount Apo—9,695 feet
LONGEST RIVER	Cagayan River—112 miles

Photosynthesis

see also: Leaf, Plant

Green plants use the energy of sunlight to make their own food. This is called photosynthesis.

How photosynthesis works

Leaves are a plant's factories for making food. The green stuff in leaves is called chlorophyll. It takes in energy from sunlight. The chlorophyll uses carbon dioxide from the air and water from the soil to make sugary food for the plant.

Oxygen is given out into the air during photosynthesis. Only green plants make their own food this way. Plants provide food for animals. Even animals that do not eat plants feed on animals that do eat plants. Animals and people could not survive without photosynthesis.

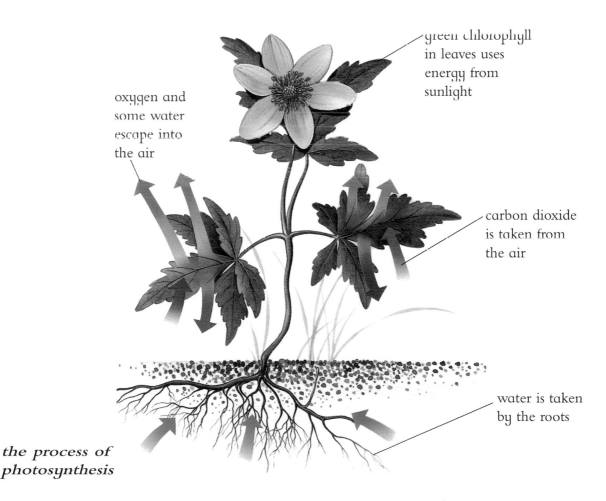

green chlorophyll in leaves uses energy from sunlight

oxygen and some water escape into the air

carbon dioxide is taken from the air

water is taken by the roots

the process of photosynthesis

Pig

see also: Mammal

A pig is a mammal. Some kinds of pigs are very hairy. Other kinds have smooth, pink skin. Farmers all over the world keep pigs for food. Bacon, pork, ham, and sausages come from pigs. Wild pigs live in some countries.

Pig families

A male pig is called a boar. A female pig is called a sow. Pig babies are called piglets. Sows on farms can have as many as 20 piglets in one litter.

Pigs once lived wild in forests. Now most pigs are kept for food. They live in farm buildings or in fields.

PIG FACTS

NUMBER OF KINDS	more than 80
COLOR	white, brown, black, red
LENGTH	5 feet
WEIGHT	up to 440 lbs.
STATUS	common
LIFE SPAN	10 years
ENEMIES	wolves, people

some pigs are bred to have big, fat bodies so there is more meat

floppy ears flap insects away

teats to feed milk to piglets

a female pig

turned up snout to search for and dig out food

This sow has a litter of seventeen piglets.

PLANT AND MEAT EATER

Pigs are scavengers. They will eat just about anything.

Pigeon

see also: Bird

A pigeon is a bird. Many kinds of pigeons live in woods, on cliffs, and in towns and cities. They live all around the world. Pigeons make a sound called cooing. Some pigeons are also called doves.

PIGEON FACTS

NUMBER OF KINDS	255
COLOR	many colors
LENGTH	up to 36 inches
WEIGHT	up to 4 lbs.
STATUS	common
LIFE SPAN	up to 15 years
ENEMIES	buzzards, falcons, martens, foxes, badgers, people

Pigeon families

Pigeons live together in big groups called flocks. Each spring a male and a female pick a nesting site. The male collects twigs and stems. He weaves a nest. The female lays two to four eggs in the nest.

A baby pigeon is called a squab. The adult pigeons feed the squabs "pigeon's milk." This is made from digested food.

strong, wide wings for flying

place where "pigeon's milk" is made

a wood pigeon

long claws on feet for holding on to branches and ledges while sleeping

These Australian crested pigeons walk into the water to drink.

PLANT EATER

A pigeon eats grain, leaves, and fruit. Sometimes large flocks of pigeons eat crops in farmers' fields. Farmers don't like pigeons.

Planet

see also: Solar System, Sun

Planets are large balls of gas and rock. Planets orbit a star. Nine planets have been discovered in our solar system. Earth is one of them. The others are Mercury, Venus, Mars, Jupiter, Saturn, Uranus, Neptune, and Pluto. Some of the other stars in the sky also have planets orbiting them.

Mercury
36 million miles from sun

Venus
67 million miles from sun

Earth
93 million miles from sun

Mars
142 million miles from sun

Jupiter
483 million miles
from sun

The nine planets

All nine planets travel around the sun. The planets near to the sun are the hottest planets. Planets far from the sun are the coldest planets. Some of the nine planets can be seen without a telescope. From Earth, these planets look like stars. Uranus, Neptune, and Pluto can only be seen with a telescope. People have never landed on another planet. Space exploration probes have landed on Mars and Venus. Space exploration probes have taken pictures of all the planets except Pluto.

Saturn
886 million miles
from sun

Uranus
1,782 million miles from sun

Neptune
2,795 million miles from sun

Pluto
3,664 million miles from sun

DID YOU KNOW?

A person who studies objects in space is called an astronomer. The study of space is called astronomy. It is the oldest science.

These are the nine planets of our solar system. The sizes of the planets are very different.

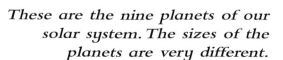

Plant

see also: Flower, Food Chain, Leaf,
Life Cycle, Photosynthesis, Seed, Stem

A plant is a living thing. It
grows and stays in one place.
Plants grow all over the world.
A person who studies plants is
called a botanist.

PLANT FACTS

NUMBER OF	
KINDS	more than 260 thousand
HEIGHT	from microscopic to 289 feet
LIFE SPAN	up to 5,000 years
ENEMIES	bacteria, insects, people

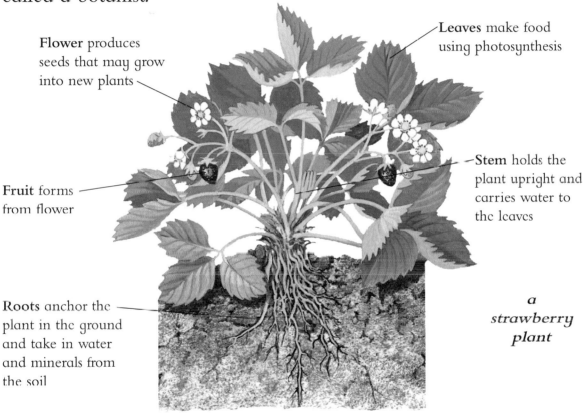

Flower produces
seeds that may grow
into new plants

Leaves make food
using photosynthesis

Fruit forms
from flower

Stem holds the
plant upright and
carries water to
the leaves

Roots anchor the
plant in the ground
and take in water
and minerals from
the soil

a
strawberry
plant

The life of a plant

Most plants grow from seeds. Seeds are
made in the flowers of the parent plant.
Some plants, such as ferns and mosses,
grow from spores. All plants need water,
sunlight, and nutrients from the soil to
grow. Different kinds of plants grow best
in different places. Plants grow in forests,
deserts, fields, and even in the oceans.

People and plants

Plants provide people with food,
medicines, and many useful materials.
Rubber, cotton, paper, rope, and wood
are just some of the materials that
come from plants. Plants also give
all animals oxygen to breathe. Plants
take the carbon dioxide out of the air.
They put oxygen into the air.

Plastic

see also: Heat

Plastic is a man-made material. It can be formed into many shapes. Most plastic is made from chemicals found in oil. Some plastics are hard. Some plastics are bendable. Most plastics are lighter than metals.

Making things from plastic

Plastics are easy to shape by molding. A mold is an empty shape. A liquid can be poured into the shape. Plastic is melted and pushed or sucked into molds. When it cools, it hardens and keeps the shape of the mold. Plastic can also be used to make thread and fibers to make cloth. Nylon, rayon, and polyester are plastic fabrics.

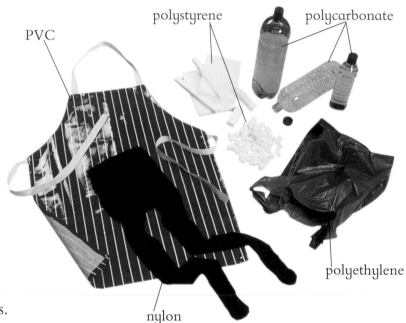

PVC

polystyrene

polycarbonate

polyethylene

nylon

Different types of plastic are used to make different things.

Recycling plastic

Plastic does not rot or corrode. Plastic objects that are thrown away stay in the dump sites.

Supplies of oil are running out. Some plastics can be melted down and used again to save oil. The plastic in plastic drink bottles and other plastic containers can be used again in this way. This is called recycling.

DID YOU KNOW?

One of the first plastics used was invented in 1908. It was invented by a Belgian who moved to the United States. His name was Leo Hendrik Baekeland. The plastic he invented was called Bakelite. It broke easily, so it is no longer used.

Platypus

see also: Mammal

A platypus is an unusual mammal. It has a bill like a bird and it lays eggs. It also has fur like most mammals. The platypus lives only in Australia.

Platypus families

Each platypus digs a tunnel in a river bank. It lives on its own. The female platypus digs a long tunnel each autumn. She lays two or three eggs in it. She holds the eggs with her tail to keep them warm until they hatch. She feeds her babies on milk as other mammals do. The babies stay in their mother's tunnel until they are four to five months old.

PLATYPUS FACTS

NUMBER OF KINDS	1
COLOR	brown
LENGTH	about 24 inches
WEIGHT	about 4 lbs.
STATUS	rare
LIFE SPAN	not known
ENEMIES	pollution in water

thick, waterproof fur for swimming

a platypus

nostrils, eyes, and ears close to keep water out when swimming

wide, webbed front paws for fast swimming and claws for digging

bill for picking up food from the bottom of rivers and streams

This platypus is digging food from the bottom of a river.

INSECT AND MEAT EATER

A platypus eats insect larvae, water snails, and crayfish. It collects food from the river surface and floor. It puts the food in its cheek pouches. When its pouches are full, it brings the food to the surface to eat.

Pledge of Allegiance

The Pledge of Allegiance is a promise Americans make to be loyal to their country. A pledge is a kind of promise. Allegiance is another word for loyalty.

The story of the Pledge

The Pledge of Allegiance was written by Francis Bellamy. He wrote it in 1892 for the 400th anniversary of Christopher Columbus's first voyage to America. That year, children in schools said the Pledge to celebrate Columbus Day.

Changing with the times

The Pledge of Allegiance has changed since 1892. At first, people pledged allegiance to "my flag." Later, the words "United States of America" were added. In 1954, the words "under God" were added to the Pledge. Some people say those words should not have been added because they go against the ideas of the Constitution. The Constitution says government and religion should always be separate.

Students from Amido Elementary School, Washington, D.C., recite the Pledge of Allegiance.

THE PLEDGE OF ALLEGIANCE

I pledge allegiance to the flag of the United States of America and to the republic for which it stands, one nation under God, indivisible, with liberty and justice for all.

Saying the Pledge

In 1942, Congress officially approved the Pledge of Allegiance. Americans say the Pledge at school, at public gatherings, and on important occasions. When Americans say the Pledge of Allegiance, they should stand with their right hand over their heart. They should face the American flag.

Poetry

see also: Literature

Poetry tells a story or describes feelings. Poetry uses words in verses. It is a kind of literature. A single piece of poetry is called a poem. A person who writes poetry is called a poet.

The first poems

The first poems were really songs. The words were sung or spoken to music. About 2,500 years ago, people started writing and speaking verses without music. They still kept the rhythms and musical sounds. Many cultures all over the world write, speak, and sing poetry.

HENRY WADSWORTH LONGFELLOW (1807–1882)

Longfellow was an American poet. He helped to make poetry popular. Most of Longfellow's poems were long. They told stories. His most famous poem is *The Song of Hiawatha*. It is a very long poem about a Native American chief. The rhythm of the poem is like Native American music and dances.

DID YOU KNOW?

Poetry can tell a story. A poem can have characters to help tell the story.

A.A. MILNE (1882–1956)

A.A. Milne wrote poems and stories for his son, Christopher Robin. He used Christopher Robin and Christopher's toys as characters in his writing. His two books of poetry are *When We Were Very Young* and *Now We Are Six*.

A. A. Milne, his son Christopher Robin, and the teddy bear, Pooh.

What makes a poem?

There are many different kinds of poetry. Some poems have words that rhyme. Most poems have a rhythm. The rhythm is made with strong and weak sounds. This kind of rhythm is called meter.

Poland

see also: Europe

Poland is a country in central Europe. It is mostly lowlands with hills. There are mountains in the south. The only coast is in the north. Summers are warm. Winters are cold.

Living in Poland

More than half of the people in Poland live in cities and large towns. Some people work in mines. They dig out coal, copper, silver, lead, zinc, and sulfur. Other people make things like ships and machinery. The things they make are sold to other countries. Farmers grow grains, potatoes, sugar beets, and fruits. Some farmers raise cattle and pigs.

Polish people have many traditional foods. Pancakes and rich cream cakes are favorites. People also enjoy thin pork sausages called *kabanosy*. These sausages are cooked in a creamy sauce.

Traditional national costumes are sometimes worn at Poland's many folksong festivals.

DID YOU KNOW?

Every year a Midsummer Night Festival is held in the city of Warsaw. It is held on June 23. Candles decorated with flowers are floated down the river during the festival.

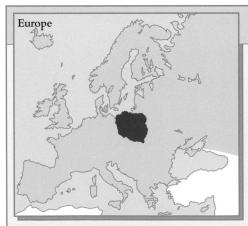

Europe

FACT FILE

PEOPLE	Polish, Poles
POPULATION	almost 39 million
MAIN LANGUAGE	Polish
CAPITAL CITY	Warsaw
MONEY	Zloty
HIGHEST MOUNTAIN	Rysy—8,199 feet
LONGEST RIVER	Vistula River—675 miles

Pollution

see also: Air, Ocean, Road

Pollution is when something is made dirty or damaged. It can be caused by spilling or dumping waste. Pollution can look bad, smell awful, sound noisy, or be unhealthy. It can damage or kill plants, wildlife, and even people.

KINDS OF POLLUTION

Air pollution comes from car and truck exhaust and factories.

Sea pollution is caused by accidents to oil tankers and other ships, things dumped overboard, and sewage and chemicals pumped from the land into the sea or ocean.

Water pollution is caused when rain washes chemicals used on farms into streams and rivers. Some factories dump waste liquids into streams and rivers.

Litter is trash that is dumped in the streets, into water, and in buildings.

Noise pollution can be caused by truck and airplane engines. Other loud noises also add to noise pollution.

Light pollution is caused by the bright lights of some towns and cities, making it impossible to see the stars in the night sky.

In 1989 an oil tanker ran onto land in Alaska. It caused a lot of damage. The oil polluted the water and the shore. It killed animals and plant life.

These trees in Poland have been killed by acid rain. Acid rain is caused when pollution in the air makes rainwater bad.

Pop Music

see also: Music, Musical Instrument

"Pop music" is short for popular music. Pop music is any kind of music created for as many people as possible to hear and enjoy. Pop music is usually lively. It will have catchy tunes and strong rhythms.

The first pop music

Popular music has changed many times. The first pop music in English-speaking countries was the ballads sung in taverns. Funny or romantic songs were sung in theaters and music halls. Pop music changed as new ideas and fashions came into the music. African-American music, different dance music, and many other styles spread around the world. Pop music today often has simple rhythms and melodies. The words are usually easy to remember.

Pop songs are usually less than four minutes long. One or more people sing. The music is usually played on electrically amplified instruments.

BILL HALEY (1927–1981)

One of the first performers of modern pop music was Bill Haley. He was a composer, bandleader, singer, and guitarist. Bill Haley recorded a song called "Rock Around the Clock" in 1956. He sang with his group, the Comets. The song was about dancing all night long. It was based on African-American music. Haley's group played with a fast beat. They played drums and electric guitars. This style of music is called rock and roll.

This pop group called Hanson is made up of three brothers.

Porcupine

see also: Mammal

A porcupine is a mammal. It has a coat of sharp spines. The spines are called quills. There are two main kinds of porcupines. The African porcupine lives on the ground. The North American porcupine climbs trees.

Porcupine families

The female African porcupine has two litters a year. Each litter has two or three babies. The female North American porcupine only has one baby a year. Male porcupines do not help care for the babies. The mothers feed their babies milk for a few weeks. Then the babies start feeding themselves.

PORCUPINE FACTS

NUMBER OF KINDS	22
COLOR	brown or black
LENGTH	up to 32 inches
WEIGHT	up to 60 lbs.
STATUS	common
LIFE SPAN	up to 15 years
ENEMIES	African—leopards, lions, people North American—pine martens, people

an African porcupine

long, sharp spines for keeping enemies away

hairless pads on front paws for holding food and branches

sharp claws for gripping and climbing

It is unusual to see porcupines during the day.

PLANT EATER

Both types of porcupine eat at night. African porcupines eat roots. North American tree-climbing porcupines like to eat young leaves and tree bark. Porcupines hold food with their front paws. Then they nibble their food.

Port

see also: Bay, Coast, Ship

A port is a place on or near land. It is where ships can tie up or drop anchor. The tie-up place is called the docks. Ships stay in port until they are ready to sail again.

Types of port

Some ports are for ships that carry passengers. Many of these are ports for ferryboats. There are also ports for cargo ships. These ports need cranes, conveyor belts, and pipelines to handle the goods.

A port needs to be safe from big waves. A port can be a harbor in a bay. It can be where a river comes out to sea. The water must be deep enough for the ships. Some ports have big gates to keep the water in when the tide goes out. These are called lock gates.

Seattle, Washington, is an important port city. This is a view of its shipyard.

This is the port in Rotterdam in the Netherlands. Cargo comes in huge containers. The containers are lifted by cranes from the ships to the trucks on the docks.

People and ports

Many people work in ports. Some people build and repair ships. Other people are dock workers, customs officers, and truck drivers. Many of the world's biggest coastal cities have ports. These cities are big because goods come in and out through their ports.

DID YOU KNOW?

More ships come and go from the port of Rotterdam in the Netherlands than any other port in the world. The city of Rotterdam is located where the Rhine River enters the North Sea.

Portugal

see also: Europe

Portugal is a country in southwest Europe. There are mountains to the north. There is dry, flat land in the center. The far south has hot summers. Portugal's winters are mild.

Living in Portugal

Many Portuguese live in villages. Many houses are painted white in the south. The color white reflects the sunlight and keeps the houses cool. Portugal sells cork from trees and canned fish to other countries. Factories make clothes, shoes, and paper. Grain, olives, and grapes are grown on farms. Sheep, cattle, and pigs are also raised.

Salt cod is the national dish. This is codfish that has been salted and dried. It is served with salad, potatoes, and olive oil.

Traditional songs are popular. Each town has its own Christian saint's day festival.

Local folk dances are often danced to accordion music.

DID YOU KNOW?

Portugal had many famous explorers. Europe's first school of astronomy and navigation opened in Portugal in 1435.

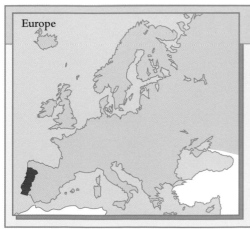

Europe

FACT FILE

PEOPLE	Portuguese
POPULATION	about 10 million
MAIN LANGUAGE	Portuguese
CAPITAL CITY	Lisbon
MONEY	Euro
HIGHEST MOUNTAIN	Estrela—6,539 feet
LONGEST RIVER	Tagos (or Tajo) River—626 miles

Praying Mantis

see also: Insect, Invertebrate

The praying mantis is an insect. It has a long, thin body. Its body is about the size of an adult's finger. A praying mantis holds its strong front legs up in front of its head when it is hunting. It looks as if it is praying. It lives in many warm countries.

How the praying mantis lives

The male praying mantis is smaller than the female. The female often eats the male after they mate. The female lays her eggs on a plant. The eggs hatch into live insects.

PRAYING MANTIS FACTS

NUMBER OF KINDS	over 2,000
COLOR	green or brown
LENGTH	up to 8 inches
STATUS	becoming rare
ENEMIES	birds, people

feelers and eyes to smell and see

shape and coloring for hiding from enemies and for hiding while hunting

a praying mantis

strong, spiny front legs grab food and keep it from wriggling free

INSECT EATER

The praying mantis sits very still when it hunts. Its powerful front legs are ready for an insect to come close. Then it quickly grabs the insect and eats it alive.

These young praying mantises have just hatched live from their eggs.

Pterosaur

see also: Dinosaur, Fossil

The pterosaurs were flying lizards. They lived at the time of the dinosaurs. They had leathery wings. They did not have feathers. Their long, bony tails helped them steer. There were many kinds of pterosaur.

Lifestyle

Some pterosaurs were small and fast flying. The pterodactyl was a small pterosaur. Other pterosaurs were giants. Their wings were 23 feet across. They were as big as a small airplane. The giant pteranodon could swoop down. It could scoop up fish from rivers or lakes. Pterodactyls may have also been able to catch flying insects.

FACTS

COLOR... not known
SIZE....... from 8 inches to 36 feet
WEIGHT . up to 55 lbs.
BIGGEST .. Quetzalcoatlus–
36 feet long

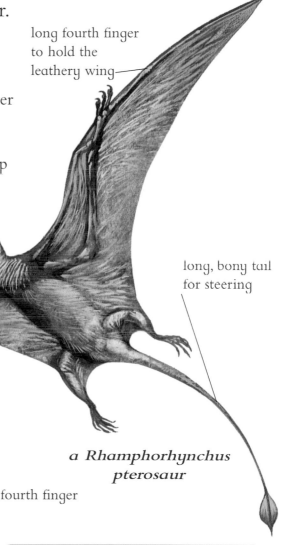

long fourth finger to hold the leathery wing

long, bony tail for steering

a Rhamphorhynchus pterosaur

fourth finger

This is a fossil of a Dimorphodon pterosaur. It shows the long fourth finger bone.

INSECT AND MEAT EATER

Pterosaurs had rows of spiky teeth. This helped them to catch fish and insects.

Puerto Rico

see also: North America,
United States of America

Puerto Rico is a country in the Caribbean Sea. It is a group of islands. The largest island has mountains. The north and south coasts have flat land. The climate is warm, windy, and wet.

Living in Puerto Rico

Most people in Puerto Rico live in the cities and towns. They work in factories and offices. The work of some Puerto Ricans is helping tourists. Coffee, vegetables, sugar cane, rice, and bananas are grown on farms.

Puerto Ricans are a mixture of African, Spanish, and local Native Americans. Most of the people are Roman Catholic Christians. There are many colorful religious festivals and saints' days. One of the most important festivals is "Festival of Innocents." Costumes and floats are used in the celebration.

This man is wearing a special festival costume. He has won a prize.

DID YOU KNOW?

Puerto Rico has a special relationship with the United States. Its representative in the U.S. Congress can speak, but cannot vote.

North America

FACT FILE

PEOPLE	Puerto Ricans
POPULATION	almost 4 million
MAIN LANGUAGES	Spanish, English
CAPITAL CITY	San Juan
MONEY	U.S. dollar
HIGHEST MOUNTAIN	Cerro de Punta—4,391 feet
LONGEST RIVER	Grand de Arecibo—40 miles

Puppetry

see also: Drama, Theater

Puppetry is a way of telling stories. It uses dolls called puppets. The person who moves them is called a puppeteer.

Types of puppets

Puppets can be moved in different ways. A puppeteer might wear a glove puppet on his or her hand. Puppets can also be moved with strings or on sticks. They can even be moved electronically. Some puppets are cut from flat shapes. A light shines from behind them. These puppets appear as shadows.

How puppets are used

Puppets are often used to tell stories to children. In some countries, such as Japan, puppet shows are also for adults.

Puppets are still a popular way of telling a story. New puppet shows are performed for live audiences and for television. One famous puppeteer is Jim Henson. He created the Muppets. Another famous puppeteer is Gerry Anderson. He invented the puppets in many space adventure stories.

The children are watching a Punch and Judy show. It is about Punch and his wife, Judy. In these stories, Punch fights with Judy, a policeman, and a crocodile. Punch fights with everyone.

Puppets from the island of Java in Indonesia are used to tell folktales. They are moved by sticks.

DID YOU KNOW?

Puppets that hang from strings are called marionettes.

Pyramid

see also: Egypt; Egypt, Ancient; Maya

Pyramids were first made by the ancient Egyptians. They built these buildings about 4,500 years ago. The first pyramids had square bases. The sides went up to a point. They looked like steps. Later pyramids had smooth sides.

What were the pyramids?

The pyramids were huge tombs. They were built for the ancient Egyptian rulers. These rulers were called pharaohs. The ancient Egyptians believed people would have a life after they died. So they buried their dead with food and useful things.

The Egyptian pyramids were so well built that they are still standing.

KEY DATES

2660 B.C.	first step pyramid is built in ancient Egypt
2600 B.C.	first smooth-sided pyramid is built in ancient Egypt
2580 B.C.	Great Pyramid is built at Giza
1500 B.C.	ancient Egyptians begin to bury their pharaohs in tombs, not pyramids
A.D. 500	Maya build step pyramid temples

Mummies

Ancient Egyptians believed people needed their bodies after they died. So, they tried to make sure that dead bodies did not rot away. They took out the soft insides of the dead person. Next they dried out the body. Then they wrapped the body in bandages that were soaked in oil.

A body that got this special treatment is called a mummy. The dried mummy was put in a specially shaped wooden box. A face was painted on the box. The face looked like the person inside the box. This special box is called a sarcophagus.

DID YOU KNOW?

The Maya people of Central America built step pyramids. The pyramids were temples to their gods. People climbed the steps to get to the temple on the flat top.

Rabbit

see also: Hare, Mammal

A rabbit is a small, long-eared mammal. It is often kept as a pet. A rabbit can run very fast. Some kinds of rabbits can run as fast as 25 miles per hour. They can hop a long way in one leap. A rabbit usually sleeps in the day. It comes out at night. Rabbits live all around the world.

Rabbit families

Some kinds of rabbits live with many other rabbits. They live in large underground tunnels called a warren. Some kinds of rabbits live alone.

A male is called a buck. A female is called a doe. A baby is sometimes called a kitten or a bunny. Female rabbits have several litters each year. They have five to eight babies in each litter. Some rabbits have their babies underground. Other rabbits make nests in the grass.

These bunnies are six days old. They have not opened their eyes yet.

RABBIT FACTS

NUMBER OF KINDS	44 rabbits and hares
COLOR	brownish-gray; pet rabbits can be many colors
LENGTH	up to 24 inches
WEIGHT	up to 11 lbs.
STATUS	common
LIFE SPAN	up to 6 years
ENEMIES	foxes, snakes, eagles, people

sensitive nose to smell friends and enemies

long ears to listen for danger

a European rabbit

strong back legs for hopping and running

PLANT EATER

A rabbit eats mostly grass, clover, and herbs. In winter the rabbit eats bark, twigs, and seeds. Rabbits that live near the sea eat seaweed.

Raccoon

see also: Mammal

A raccoon is a furry mammal. It has black stripes around its tail and a black face mask. Raccoons live near trees and water. They live in North and South America. Raccoons can swim and climb well.

Raccoon families

The female raccoon has as many as three babies. They are called kits. The mother feeds the kits milk. She teaches the older kits to fish with their front paws.

In summer, some raccoons live on their own. Some live in small groups. A group is a mother raccoon and her kits. In winter, raccoons crowd together in dens to keep warm.

RACCOON FACTS

NUMBER OF KINDS	1
COLOR	gray and black
LENGTH	up to 3 feet
WEIGHT	up to 33 lbs.
STATUS	common
LIFE SPAN	up to 10 years
ENEMIES	people

sharp teeth for tearing food and crushing crab shells

a raccoon

tail for balance while climbing

hands for feeling and gripping

These kits are staying near their den.

MEAT EATER

Raccoons usually come out at night. They hunt for eggs in trees. They hunt for crabs, frogs, and fish in water. Raccoons are wild animals, but they often live near people. They move into areas where people have their houses. They search through garbage cans for food.

Radio

see also: Communication, Television

Radio is an important way to communicate. Radio uses radio waves. The radio waves are sent from a transmitter to a receiver. Receivers are usually radios like the ones in cars and homes.

The first radio

The first radio was made by Guglielmo Marconi in 1895. Then in 1901, Marconi discovered how to send a radio signal across the Atlantic Ocean. He sent the signal from England to the United States. After a few years, most big ships had radios. A ship with a radio could send a message if it was in trouble. By the 1920s, people were listening to news, music, and entertainment on their own radios.

This is a radio tower in Australia. Radio towers are very tall so that the signals they send are not blocked by hills or buildings.

How radios work

Each radio signal has a different frequency. The frequency is the number of radio waves that arrive in one second. A person is choosing a frequency when he or she chooses to listen to a radio program.

DID YOU KNOW?

Televisions and cellular telephones use radio signals. Communication satellites receive radio signals from one place on Earth. They bounce the signals back to another place on Earth.

This radio receiver is powered by batteries. Small battery radios were first available in 1955.

Railroad

see also: Train, Transportation

A railroad is a track on which trains travel. Railroads connect cities, factories, and ports. They carry people and goods.

The first railroads

The first railroads were built 200 years ago. They had wooden tracks. Horses pulled boxes of coal along the tracks. Then the steam engine was invented. It was powerful. It could work much faster than horses or people. Railroads became longer and connected more places. They carried more people. Today, some railroads go through mountain tunnels. Some railroads even go under the sea.

People and railroads

People could travel a long way very quickly on railroads. Goods could get to places far from where they were made. Fresh food could travel long distances in short amounts of time. Cities and towns grew because they were connected by railroads.

RAILROAD FACTS

FIRST PUBLIC
RAILROAD . . . . opened in 1825 between Stockton and Darlington (England)

LONGEST ROUTE . . . 5,860 miles from Moscow to Nakhodka in Russia

BIGGEST STATION . . Grand Central Station in New York City has 67 tracks on two levels

The last spike was driven into this track on May 10, 1869. This completed the railroad line that crossed the United States.

This modern, electric-powered train travels at high speeds. The tracks are made especially for high-speed trains.

Rain Forest

see also: Forest, Plant

Rain forests are very important for the earth. Many different plants and animals live in rain forests. Many of these plants and animals are useful to people. Most rain forests are in hot, wet, tropical areas.

Tropical rain forests

Tropical rain forests have five layers. The bottom layer has small plants, such as mosses and ferns. It also has rich soil made of rotted leaves. Small animals and insects live in the bottom layer. The next layer is shrubs and larger ferns. The third layer is the young trees.

The next layer is the canopy. It is thick and green and about 100 feet high. It is the tops of fully grown trees. The last layer is a few very tall trees. They poke up through the canopy. This layer is called the emergent layer.

Temperate rain forests

There are cool, wet, temperate rain forests in some parts of the United States, Europe, Australia, and Africa. The trees are mainly the type that lose their leaves in winter.

This cool, damp, temperate rain forest is in the state of Washington.

This tropical rain forest is along the Amazon River in Brazil. Different plants and animals live in each layer.

DID YOU KNOW?

Much of the world's rain forests are being cut down. An area nearly as big as Louisiana is cut down every year. If this continues, there will be no rain forests.

Rainbow

see also: Color, Light

A rainbow is an arch of seven different colors.
A rainbow happens when white sunlight shines
through raindrops. The white light is split into
different colors. These colors are called the color
spectrum of light.

How is a rainbow made?

All the colors of a rainbow are in
sunlight. Light from the sun is seen as
white light. It is really made up of red,
orange, yellow, green, blue, indigo, and
violet light.

Sunlight bends when it hits a raindrop.
Each color of light bends a little bit
differently. The colors separate. They
form a spectrum.

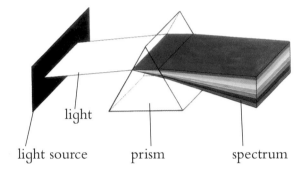

light

light source   prism   spectrum

*A raindrop acts like a prism. When
the sunlight hits the raindrop, the
light is divided into colors.*

How to see a rainbow

A rainbow only appears when the sun
is low in the sky during a rain shower.
To see the rainbow, turn so that the sun
is behind you. Look straight ahead. The
lower the sun is, the bigger the rainbow
arch will be.

DID YOU KNOW?

You can never find the place where
a rainbow comes to the ground. This
is because a rainbow is a trick of the
light. A rainbow can only be seen
from a distance.

*This rainbow will fade away when
the rain stops falling or when the
sun goes behind clouds.*

Rat

see also: Mammal

A rat is a quick, four-legged mammal. Rats are clever. They can learn to live anywhere. Rats have followed humans around the world. They live in cities and houses where it is warm. They live where there is plenty of food. Rats also live in rural areas. They can spread diseases that can kill people.

Rat families

Rats have many babies. One pair of rats can have hundreds of babies in its lifetime. The female can have a litter three times a year. There might be as many as fourteen babies in each litter. The female feeds the babies milk. The babies look for their own food when they are old enough. In rural areas, rats live in groups called colonies.

strong, hairless, muscular tail for balance

This Acacia rat from Botswana, Africa, lives with her family in a tree.

RAT FACTS

NUMBER OF	
KINDS	1,082 mice and rats
COLOR	usually brown or gray
LENGTH	up to 20 inches
STATUS	common
LIFE SPAN	up to 5 years
ENEMIES	dogs, cats, people

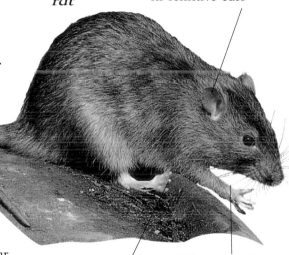

a brown rat

large flaps protect its sensitive ears

claws and strong legs for running and climbing

whiskers feel the sides of small spaces to keep the rat from getting trapped

PLANT AND MEAT EATER

Rats have front teeth that never stop growing. The teeth sharpen themselves as they wear down. Rats eat grain, fruit, rubbish, and scraps. They often steal food from humans. They also get into food that is being stored.

Ray

see also: Fish, Sea Life

A ray is a special kind of fish. It does not have fins. A ray has a flat body with wide wings. It swims through the water by flapping its wings. Rays live in oceans around the world. Some rays have poisonous stings on their tails. The stings protect them.

Ray families

Big rays swim alone in the sea. Manta rays are big rays. Smaller rays gather close together in groups. Stingrays are small rays. Rays do not have homes. Some rays spend a lot of time hiding in the sand on the bottom of the sea. Female rays do not lay eggs. They give birth to about ten live babies. The babies look after themselves as soon as they are born.

RAY FACTS

NUMBER OF KINDS	425
COLOR	different colors on top, white underneath
LENGTH	up to 16 feet
WEIGHT	manta ray—up to 3,000 lbs.
STATUS	common
LIFE SPAN	up to 20 years
ENEMIES	people

wings for swimming

bendable tail with poisonous sting

a stingray

eyes on the top of the head for seeing things when hiding in sand

flat body for hiding in sand

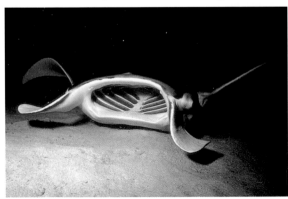

This manta ray has its mouth open. The filter plates inside catch small animals in the water.

PLANT AND MEAT EATER

Manta rays eat shrimp, plankton, and small fish that they filter from the water. Stingrays eat sea worms, shellfish, and crabs.

Reptile

see also: Animal

A reptile is a cold-blooded animal with scaly skin. Snakes, crocodiles, lizards, and tortoises are kinds of reptiles. Reptiles live on land and in water. They live all around the world, but not in the coldest places.

Types of reptiles

The four main groups of reptiles are:

Alligators and crocodiles – These are the largest reptiles.

Lizards and snakes – There are more than 5,000 kinds of lizards and snakes around the world. This is the biggest group of reptiles.

Tortoises and turtles – These are protected by their hard shells. The shell of the Galapagos giant tortoise can be 5 feet long.

Tuataras – These are very rare. Tuataras live only on North Island in New Zealand.

INSECT AND MEAT EATER

All reptiles are hunters. They eat meat, fish, and insects. Reptiles do not use their energy to heat their blood, so they do not eat much. Many reptiles can go without food for months or even years.

REPTILE FACTS

NUMBER OF KINDS	more than 6,000
LONGEST-LIVED	tortoises, up to 200 years
LARGEST	leatherback turtle, 1,658 lbs.

This is a tuatara from New Zealand.

This Wheeler's Gecko is a type of lizard. It has sticky pads on its feet. It can crawl up and down vertical surfaces.

Rhinoceros

see also: Mammal

A rhinoceros is a large, horned mammal. A rhinoceros is also called a rhino. Its thick skin is like armor. Three kinds of rhinos live in Asia. These rhinos have only one horn. They are very rare rhinos. Two kinds of rhinos live in Africa. These rhinos have two horns.

RHINOCEROS FACTS

NUMBER OF KINDS	5
COLOR	gray
HEIGHT	up to 7 feet
LENGTH	up to 12 feet
WEIGHT	up to 4,850 lbs.
STATUS	endangered
LIFE SPAN	20 to 50 years
ENEMIES	lions, hyenas, tigers, people

Rhinoceros families

A rhinoceros lives by itself. It lives on grasslands. It shares a waterhole or mud wallow with other rhinos. A male rhino is called a bull. A female is called a cow. A baby is called a calf. A cow has one calf at a time. She looks after her calf for two to five years. Bulls fight over territory, but they let females and calves into their areas.

sensitive ears for hearing enemies and other rhinos

large horn for fighting and protection

a white rhinoceros

upper lip for pulling up plants

thick skin for protection

PLANT EATER

A rhinoceros eats branches, leaves, fruit, grass, and herbs.

This female rhinoceros is feeding her calf. She has a very long horn.

Rhode Island

see also: United States of America

Rhode Island is a state in the northeastern United States of America. It is not really an island. Rhode Island is the smallest state in the nation. There are rocky cliffs and sandy beaches. The weather is mild. In winter, there is snow on the higher land in the western part of the state.

People come to Rhode Island to sail and swim.

Life in Rhode Island

Rhode Island has many manufacturing industries for its small size. Jewelry, silverware, and toys are important products. Factories also make textiles, electronic equipment, and boats of all sizes.

> ## DID YOU KNOW?
> Rhode Island's real name is State of Rhode Island and Providence Plantations.

The state has a large bay called Narragansett Bay. There are islands in the bay. The coast and ocean provide jobs for workers in Rhode Island. People work in the ports. Some people fish along the coast. They catch bass, tuna, flounder, and lobsters. Other workers look after the many visitors who come to Rhode Island's shores.

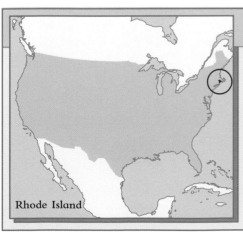

Rhode Island

FACT FILE

BECAME A STATE...	1790 (13th state)
LAND AREA.........	1,045 square miles (50th largest land area)
POPULATION	1,076,164 (43rd most populated state)
OTHER NAME......	Ocean State
CAPITAL CITY......	Providence

River

see also: Delta, Flood, Valley

A river is a flow of water that drains the land. Rivers carry water from the land to the sea. A small river is called a stream.

Why rivers flow

The water in rivers comes from rain and melting snow. Some rivers begin at a lake or marsh in the mountains. Others start at a spring. A spring is where water flows out from under the ground.

Streams and rivers flow into each other to make bigger rivers. These smaller streams and rivers are called tributaries. Rivers wash away soil and rocks. Rivers make valleys.

People and rivers

People use rivers for drinking water and for watering crops. They also use rivers for bathing, washing clothes, fishing, and traveling. Fast-flowing rivers and waterfalls can be used to make electricity.

DID YOU KNOW?

The river with the most flowing water is the Amazon River in South America. The Amazon is nearly 4,000 miles long.

Some rivers make large bends or loops. The loops are called meanders.

People fish in rivers for food and for fun.

Road

see also: Transportation

A road is a pathway used by people to get from one place to another. Some roads follow paths made thousands of years ago. Most roads are new.

The first roads

Early roads were simple paths used by people and animals. They were usually the shortest or easiest way to go from one place to another. These roads were hard, dirt roads. They were made by people's footsteps packing down the dirt. These roads turned to mud when it rained.

The ancient Romans built the first road system. These roads were hard and level. They were easy to use in all weather. They were made for soldiers to walk on. Today's roads are made for wheeled vehicles, such as buses, cars, and trucks.

People and roads

Most people use roads every day. Roads make travel easy, but the traffic can cause air pollution. Roads are also expensive to design, build, and repair.

DID YOU KNOW?

The ancient Roman roads were always built as straight as possible.

ROAD FIRSTS

FIRST RECOGNIZED ROAD	Persia, 3500 B.C.
FIRST PAVED ROAD	England, 1835
FIRST FREEWAY	Italy, 1924

This is a turnpike road in England from long ago. People had to pay to use turnpikes. The money they paid was used to repair the roads.

Some modern road systems are complicated. The roads that go over the top are called overpasses. The roads that go underneath are called underpasses.

Robot

see also: Laser, Space Exploration

A robot is a machine. It works automatically or by remote control. Most robots are used in factories. They do tiresome, heavy, or dangerous jobs.

How robots work

A robot is programmed to do a certain job. This means that the instructions for the job are usually in a computer program. The robot stores the program. Then it will do the same job again and again. The robot's program must be changed if it is to do a different job.

Robots and space exploration

Robots can go on very long journeys through space. They can continue to

One day robots may be as clever as these movie robots. C3PO and R2D2 were in the movie Star Wars.

work in places where people would die. Robot space probes have gone to almost every planet in the solar system. They have not gone to Pluto yet.

Many robots have an "arm" that can hold a tool. The tool may be a paint sprayer or a welder. Many cars made in factories are painted by robots.

DID YOU KNOW?

Scientists are trying to make robots that can be programmed to think. When a computer or robot thinks, it is called "artificial intelligence."

Rock

see also: Metal, Mining

Rocks are the solid, non-living things that make up the earth. Rocks take many millions of years to form. They are on the ground and under the ground. Rocks are everywhere in the world. There are many different types of rock. Some rocks are hard. Other rocks are soft.

The three kinds of rock

Igneous rock There is no solid rock deep inside the earth. There is only a hot liquid called magma. Igneous rocks are formed when magma comes near the surface or erupts from a volcano. The hot magma cools down. It becomes solid. Igneous rocks are usually hard rocks. They do not wear away quickly.

Sedimentary rock These soft rocks were mostly formed in lakes or oceans. Some rocks were made from layers of sand or mud. Other rocks were made from the tiny shells of lake or sea creatures. It took millions of years to press them into rock.

Metamorphic rock Sedimentary rock turns into metamorphic rock when it is heated and pressed together. Metamorphic rocks are usually harder than sedimentary rocks.

These chalk cliffs are sedimentary rock. They were eroded by the sea.

DID YOU KNOW?

Rocks are made of minerals. Some minerals are metals. Iron, gold, copper, and silver are metals. Other minerals, such as salt, sulfur, and quartz, are not metals.

Slate is a metamorphic rock. It was made from layers of heated mud. Slate can be split and used on roofs.

Romania

see also: Europe

Romania is a country in southeast Europe. It has a coast along the Black Sea. The middle of Romania has mountains. The Danube River flows through the south. The winter weather is cold and dry. The summers are warm. Deer and wild boar live in the big forests.

Living in Romania

About one-third of the people work on farms. Farmers grow wheat, corn, sugar beets, and vegetables. They raise herds of cattle and sheep.

Romanians make goods from chemicals, cement, and metals. Pollution from factories is a problem in Romania.

Stories about Count Dracula come from this part of southern Romania called Transylvania.

DID YOU KNOW?

At least 300 kinds of birds live in the delta of the Danube River. Many birds stop there when they fly south for the winter.

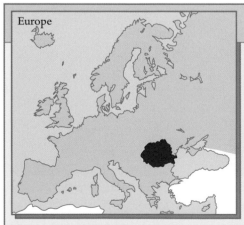

Europe

FACT FILE

PEOPLE	Romanians
POPULATION	about 22 million
MAIN LANGUAGE	Romanian
CAPITAL CITY	Bucharest
MONEY	Leu
HIGHEST MOUNTAIN	Mount Moldoveanu– 8,349 feet
LONGEST RIVER	Danube River–1,770 miles

Rome, Ancient

see also: Italy, Road

The empire of ancient Rome began with the city of Rome in Italy. Then the Romans took over other lands. They built a huge empire. The ancient Romans are known for their Latin language and their roads.

KEY DATES

753 B.C.	city of Rome begins
250 B.C.	Romans control Italy
250 B.C.–A.D.120	Romans take over more land in Europe, Asia, and North Africa
A.D. 395	Roman Empire splits into two parts

Who ruled ancient Rome?

At first, Rome was ruled by kings. Then the empire grew. It was ruled by a group of people called a Senate. Finally, the empire was ruled by an emperor. He had all the power.

What happened to ancient Rome?

The Roman Empire was at its largest in A.D.120. It was too big to be controlled from Rome. So it split into two parts. The Roman Empire became smaller as other countries and empires formed.

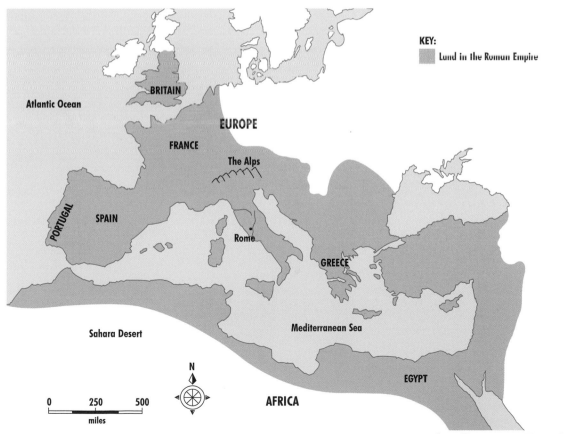

KEY:
Land in the Roman Empire

Atlantic Ocean
BRITAIN
EUROPE
FRANCE
The Alps
PORTUGAL
SPAIN
Rome
GREECE
Sahara Desert
Mediterranean Sea
N
0 250 500
miles
AFRICA
EGYPT

the Roman Empire

Roosevelt, Franklin D.

Franklin D. Roosevelt was the 32nd president of the United States of America. He helped the country get through the Great Depression. He also led the nation through World War II.

Success and illness

Roosevelt came from a rich and powerful family. His fifth cousin, Theodore Roosevelt, was the 26th president. In 1905, Roosevelt married Eleanor Roosevelt, his distant cousin. Roosevelt became a state senator in New York. Then he worked for the government in Washington, D.C. In 1921, Roosevelt became sick with polio. Being sick did not stop Roosevelt. He was elected governor of New York in 1928. In 1932, he was elected president.

Franklin D. Roosevelt

Roosevelt becomes president

Roosevelt became president during the Great Depression. Many people were homeless and had lost their jobs. Roosevelt created jobs for workers. He helped farmers who were in trouble. In 1941, the United States entered World War II. Roosevelt led the nation through the war. He served more terms than any other president.

FACT FILE

DATE OF BIRTH .... January 30, 1882
BIRTHPLACE .... Hyde Park, New York
DATE OF DEATH ... April 12, 1945
PLACE OF DEATH .. Warm Springs, Georgia
PRESIDENTIAL
NUMBER 32
DATES IN OFFICE .. 1933–1945
POLITICAL PARTY .. Democratic
VICE PRESIDENTS .. John Nance Garner,
Henry A. Wallace,
Harry S. Truman
FIRST LADY .... Eleanor Roosevelt

During the Depression, drought ruined crops all over the United States.

Roosevelt, Theodore

see also: Roosevelt, Franklin D.

Theodore Roosevelt was the 26th president of the United States of America.

Young Roosevelt

Roosevelt liked to read about wildlife and hear stories about hunting. He was sick with asthma as a child. He exercised to make himself strong.

Roosevelt attended Harvard and Columbia Universities. In 1898 he became a hero of the Spanish-American War. He was elected governor of New York.

Theodore Roosevelt's family called him "Teddy."

DID YOU KNOW?

In 1902, Roosevelt went bear hunting in Mississippi. He refused to shoot a captured bear. A New York store owner started selling toy bears. He named them "teddy bears" for Teddy Roosevelt.

Roosevelt becomes president

Roosevelt was elected as U.S. vice president in 1900. In 1901, when President William McKinley was shot, Roosevelt became president. He was the youngest person to become U.S. president. Roosevelt wanted the Panama Canal to be built across Central America. In the United States, he worked to preserve wilderness and forest lands.

This cartoon of Roosevelt is from around 1900. Roosevelt's motto was "Speak softly and carry a big stick."

FACT FILE

DATE OF BIRTH	October 27, 1858
BIRTHPLACE	New York City
DATE OF DEATH	January 9, 1919
PLACE OF DEATH	Oyster Bay, New York
PRESIDENTIAL NUMBER	26
DATES IN OFFICE	1901–1909
POLITICAL PARTY	Republican
VICE PRESIDENT	Charles W. Fairbanks
FIRST LADY	Edith Roosevelt

Root

see also: Plant

The roots of a plant are the parts that usually grow under the ground. Roots take in water. They hold the plant in the soil.

The life of a root

The root is usually the first part of a plant to grow from a seed. The tip of the root pushes down through the soil. Some plants have a large main root called a taproot. Other plants produce a network of roots. These roots grow in all directions.

Many vegetables are roots. Carrots, sweet potatoes, beets, cassava, and yams are roots. These roots store food for the plant.

All plant roots help to hold soil in place. They keep the soil from being blown away by wind or washed away by rain.

main root often stores food for the plant

root sends out branches as the plant grows bigger

the roots of a beet

tip of the root pushes down through the soil

tiny hairs take in water and minerals from the soil

DID YOU KNOW?

Some roots never go underground. Aerial roots take in water from the air. Orchids have aerial roots to hold onto bigger plants. Ivy has many small climbing roots to cling to trees and walls.